The temptation of Saint Clive

The Daily Telegraph

The 'Peterborough' Book

Selected and compiled by
MICHAEL GREEN

DAVID & CHARLES
Newton Abbot London North Pomfret (Vt)

British Library Cataloguing in Publication Data

The 'Peterborough' book.
  1. Great Britain–Social life and customs–
1945–Sources
  I. Green, Michael   II. *Daily Telegraph*
  941.085′7′08   DA588

ISBN 0–7153–8082–6

First published 1980
Second impression October 1980
Third impression November 1980
Fourth impression 1981

Typeset and printed in Great Britain
by A. Wheaton & Co Ltd Exeter
for David & Charles (Publishers) Limited
Brunel House, Newton Abbot, Devon

Published in the United States of America
by David & Charles Inc
North Pomfret, Vermont 05053, USA

Introduction

In medieval times the Abbots of Peterborough had a London hostel just off Fleet Street. They called it Peterborough Court.

The successful publishers of a newspaper called *The Daily Telegraph* moved there in the mid-nineteenth century to build and then expand their offices and printing works.

It is just over fifty years ago that the *Telegraph*, recently purchased by the first Lord Camrose, introduced a column under the heading 'London Day by Day' and over the appropriate anonym, 'Peterborough'. The final item in that first column in February 1929 was about the famously taciturn American President Coolidge and went:

> An American girl, invited to the White House, told her father that she was certain she could make Mr Coolidge talk. 'If he says three words to you, I'll give you a fur coat', said her father.
>
> On being introduced to the President, the girl explained the situation and confidently awaited the outcome. But having eyed her in silence for a minute Mr Coolidge remarked quietly, 'Poppa wins'.

In the many years since then, the final paragraph – the tailpiece, just above the 'Peterborough' signature – has become one of the best known features in any national newspaper. Only the *Financial Times* share index gets more mentions on radio, I was told when I succeeded as the latest 'Peterborough' in May 1979.

With great pleasure, I rapidly discovered the number of *Telegraph* readers willing to take the time and buy the increasingly expensive postage stamps to write to 'Peterborough' from all parts of Britain and Ireland and from every corner of the globe visited by British worker and tourist.

Every day at least a dozen letters arrive, recounting curious and comical sights and sounds or amusing tales told over tea-table and bar. Some are duplicated. I lost count of the gleeful sightings of 1979's most popular car sticker: 'Make somebody happy – wring Buzby's neck.' Some are old, indeed: there are still new viewers for 'Bill Stickers is innocent OK'.

Some are gentle, like the middle-aged man offering his seat to a lady on a bus just after the passage of the sex discrimination laws with the sad comment: 'I am afraid this is illegal.' Some are very acid, like the Yorkshireman's comment after miners' leader, Arthur Scargill, tried to put left-wing socialist principles ahead of a pay rise for his men and suffered one of his rare defeats: 'If you stand between a pig and t'trough you get your legs bitten.'

Some, I must admit, are of doubtful validity. In fact, one correspondent demanded that I put asterisks to identify any items I could not personally vouch to be gospel truth! Apart from taking a lot of fun out of life unnecessarily, who could resist the surreal beauty of the reported remark of an American tourist: 'What hurt Joe was that when we booked in here the manager had never heard of him. Back home in Winnetka he's world famous.'

If that isn't gospel, it ought to be, just like that marvellous hotel sign from Istanbul which no-one would believe but which surely existed on the second floor of the Pera Palace Hotel: 'To call room service please open door and call Room Service.'

I have made no attempt here to do an historical survey spanning 'Peterborough's' half century. The items in this book all come from the past decade. I have, however, tried to give the flavour of the column by not restricting myself entirely to the brief tailpieces: a device which, I hope, will also give readers some respite from the machine-gun like effect of staccato quips.

Some editing has been inevitable. It seemed sensible to trim the longer notes to essentials, occasionally short anecdotes have been extracted from the body of a general story and I have cut references which would have involved tedious footnote aides memoires. In a couple of cases a slight reshuffling of words has been necessary. Nothing, I believe, has been done to spoil the intent and feeling of the original.

In a concentrated collection like this, the constant repetition of the regular, daily phrases like 'a reader tells me' or 'I hear from a reader' does, I am afraid, become irritating. In many cases I have omitted it.

I say 'afraid', and I regret the omissions. For if a collection of this kind was to carry a dedication it would be to all those sharp-eyed readers who take the time to keep this little fountain of human comedy playing merrily. Long may they – and 'Peterborough,' whoever he may be – continue.

Michael Green, May 1980

Eat, Drink and Be Careful

Plate du jour
An eating house in Covent Garden – home of London
publishing – had an alluring bill of fare yesterday:
                    SPESHUL
                    QUINCHE
                    LORRIENE
                    and chips.

*From a West Country golf club bulletin: 'As in previous
years the evening concluded with a toast to the new president
in champagne provided by the retiring president, drunk as
usual at midnight'.*

Knife, fork and club
There seems to be a belligerent tone creeping into the
service in our eating establishments. In a Jersey restaurant, I hear, a notice has gone up: 'If you like home cooking – stay home.' And from Nelson, Lancashire, comes
word of the sign over the serving hatch which warns:
'Complaints to the Cook can be hazardous to your health.'

Licensing justice?
From Downside Abbey I am told that the Book of Job in
the Douai Version of the Bible contains this trial (18:
9–10) not mentioned in other translations: 'Thirst shall
burn against him. A gin is hidden for him in the earth.'

With it
Sign over a display of wine in the window of a Sussex off-
licence: 'This is the Beaune that's worth working your
fingers to.'

*A Japanese whisky, bought in Kenya, bore the label 'House
of Lords' and further declared: 'as drunk in the House of
Lords since 1066'.*

Mais oui!
A visitor to France tells me that a restaurant in Nemours
lists that famous vodka and tomato juice pick-me-up as
'Bloody Merry'.

Their own bit
From America I hear that a man and woman dining in a
Kansas City restaurant the other night were each busy

using a pocket calculator. He was keeping track of the bill and she was counting the calories.

Hard times
A café near St Paul's was offering week-end visitors a special 'Lord Mayor's Banquet'. The menu was mines-strone soup, sausages (3) and chips, bread and butter, cup of tea.

A hotel in Driffield, Yorkshire, displays a notice, for the benefit of people attending the market there, proclaiming that its licensed hours are extended through the afternoon 'on each Thursday of the year (except Sunday, Christmas Day and Good Friday)'.

Rural delights
From a Devonshire parish magazine: 'After much deliberation the judges decided that the joint winners of the best cook competition were Mrs – (an old English tart) and Miss – (a surprise hot dish).'

Downright generosity
Sign in the rear window of a car being driven by a young man in the King's Road: 'Don't drink too much on New Year's Eve. I will accompany you free of charge and drink too much for you.'

Take your pick
Seen in an Eastbourne health food shop: 'Zimbabwe live Bulgarian apricot natural goats milk yoghurt'.

Political Fringes

Political uncertainty
Mrs Thatcher has still not made up her mind whether or not to move in to No 10 Downing Street. . . . Her present home in Tite Street, Chelsea, she says, is just what she needs.

She added: 'It might prove very expensive to run two houses. I just don't know. I certainly never want to be without a home like poor old Ted was . . .'

After one or two intricate manoeuvres while skippering Great Britain II *from Greenwich to Tower Bridge, Edward*

Heath was asked whether he would like to undertake a (round-the-world) voyage like this record-breaking clipper's. 'No', he replied, 'you don't get rid of me that easily'.

Paw show

I am indebted to the *Irish Times* for a description of a disastrous house call made by Jim Molyneaux, leader of the Ulster Unionists Parliamentary party, in his Antrim constituency.

Approaching a farm-house with the intention of keeping in touch with his voters, he was greeted affectionately by a large dog which accompanied him into the house. The MP and the farmer's wife sipped tea in the immaculate parlour while the dog bounded playfully around, knocking things over and jumping with dirty paws on to the furniture.

Molyneaux was surprised that the farmer's wife did not chastise it, but also pretended not to notice the damage. The atmosphere soon began to grow inexplicably cool and he hurriedly departed.

As he walked away, Molyneaux, to his horror, heard the woman calling after him: 'Are you not going to take your dog with you?'

King Jim?

A Swanage reader tells me that her six-year-old grandson – already a keen historian – was taken to Runnymede recently. When shown the Kennedy Memorial and told that he had been President of the United States he said: 'So that's why it's called the Magna Carter.'

Essex Socialists are setting up an organisation entitled Elgar Lovers Against the Nazis (ELAN). . . . This organisation is to campaign against the use of the 'Land of Hope and Glory' words with the 'Pomp and Circumstance' No 1 March.

Norman who?

Towards the end of his speech at the Museum of the Year award lunch, Arts Minister, Norman St John Stevas, is reliably reported as saying 'But I mustn't go on singling out names . . . One must not be a name-dropper, as Her Majesty remarked to me yesterday . . .'

Uncommitted

Politicians should take note that at least one section of the electorate sees little difference between the parties. At least, that is the conclusion of Andrew Hunter, prospective Conservative Parliamentary candidate for Southampton Itchen.

While canvassing recently in Southampton's infamous red-light area Hunter inadvertently rang the bell of a house of ill-repute. When the door opened he announced that he was from the Tory party.

'That's all rights, ducks', came the reply. 'Come on in. You're all the same to us.'

Sign in the rear window of a car in Queen Victoria Street: 'The Liberal policy has no surrender value.'

Respectful visitors

A story now current in Westminster tells of a party of American tourists being guided through the Houses of Parliament when they suddenly met the dignified figure of the Lord Chancellor, Lord Hailsham, in full wig and gown. Behind them appeared the figure of Neil Marten, Conservative MP for Banbury.

'Neil!' cried the grand old man with characteristic vigour. And they did.

Ham-handed

At a reception given to open the new premises of the Anglo-Austrian Society in Queen Anne's Gate Mr Callaghan was required to pull a ribbon with Austria's Bruno Kreisky to unveil a wooden plaque marking the occasion.

'Why don't you tell us when you'd like us to pull it?' the Prime Minister genially asked the hordes of photographers. 'I'll tell you what, I'll count to five and then pull it.'

This he duly did and on the stroke of five pulled the entire plaque bodily from the wall.

Agony entrance

The White House was set for a press conference with the reporters and TV cameras in place. The executive aide intoned: 'Ladies and gentlemen, the President of the United States'.

No-one appeared and nothing was heard – except a rattling and pounding at the East Room door. . . . Several moments passed and Mr Ford appeared through another door. 'We just had a doorknob break', he explained, adding quickly: 'You can't blame that on me.'

I rather enjoyed the miscalculation of the National Front campaigner in the Thurrock by-election who hoped to address a 'factory gate' meeting outside Tilbury Docks. In twenty minutes, not a single docker left on foot and the Front was reduced to throwing leaflets at passing cars.

Porcelain philosophy
Graffitto seen in a Wolverhampton pub: 'If Labour is the answer it must have been a ruddy stupid question.'

Force-feeding
A car sticker reported from the Ilford area: 'Make your MP work. Don't re-elect him.'

Paws For Thought

A dog is a dog
The Alsatian dog still smarting from being alleged by magistrates at Southend to be an 'offensive weapon' may draw some comfort from the fact that it has not yet suffered the ultimate indignity.

That dubious honour must go to the dogs who enter the Oxford Union building where an ancient statute decrees: 'No dog shall be allowed to enter the premises unless accompanying a blind person, in which case it shall be deemed to be a cat.'

A sign spotted in a Bromley vet's waiting-room: 'Black and white kitten seeks good home – will do light mousework.'

Lasting impression
A sign in a pet shop window in New York: 'Bronze casts of your new pup's tiny paws are chumprints in the sands of time.'

There was only one dissident note during Prince Charles's visit to the Amalgamated Union of Engineering Workers' headquarters. A large hand-painted poster in the audit room said: 'Before you meet the handsome Prince you have to kiss a lot of toads.' The Prince found it hilarious; his union escort much less so.

Purr-lease
This sign was over a kitten in a basket in the window of a Birmingham pet shop: 'Get meowt of here.'

A notice in San Diego Zoo says: 'Please do not annoy, torment, pester, plague, molest, worry, badger, harry, harass, heckle, persecute, irk, bullyrag, vex, disquiet, berate, beset, bother, tease, nettle, tantalise or ruffle the animals.' Especially, may I suggest, the rare Roget's porcupinus cantankerus.

Miaow-ow!
Advertisement in a Shropshire newspaper: 'Everything for your pets. Send s.a.e. for free ill. cat.'

From America I hear that the use of pocket-sized paging devices – known as bleepers – has now been extended to pets. Apparently some dog owners have taken to attaching the receiver to the collar of their pet, so that the animal bounds home on hearing the beep.

Postbag

Staying put
In Barmouth Post Office, where there is a display of holiday postcards posted with indecipherable addresses, a new gem has been added.

It is a holiday postcard sent to Geoff, Audrey and Martin with the message: 'Having a nice time. The weather is good. The children all enjoying themselves. See you all soon. Olive, Gwyn and children.'

Written in the address section, beneath a 9p stamp, is: 'Forgot your address.'

'We know that we're good – but we're not that good', a Post Office sorter pencilled on a letter returned to the Wirral magistrates' court. It was addressed to a man at 'no fixed abode'.

Twice the letters?
In the Exeter *Express and Echo* I read that the postwoman of Cheriton Bishop, Miss Barbara Holland, has hung up her bicycle clips and retired, aged sixty-nine. Present at her farewell party were the *two men* who will take over her round (my italics).

People who complain of postal delays may be interested in a report in the correspondence columns of a Barrow-in-

Furness weekly paper from a reader who saw four Post Office vans parked on a roadside while six postmen were furiously picking mushrooms in a nearby field.

Two for the price

The postman bringing letters to a Derbyshire vicarage was asked if there was now to be only one daily delivery. 'Oh no,' he said confidently, 'you're still getting two deliveries a day but we bring them both together'.

Cheep and nasty

A car sticker seen in South London: 'Make somebody happy – wring Buzby's neck.'

Goal, Bet and Match

Numbers game

From Surrey comes the sad story of a man who arranged to go to Haydock races last Saturday and dreamed for several nights beforehand of the number seven.

He thought his guardian angel might be trying to tell him something, so when the seventh race came he put all he could afford on horse No 7, Haywire.

It came seventh.

No strikers

I hear that a recent football match between the young men of Stonesfield village near Oxford and a team from British Leyland, Cowley, had to be abandoned because only half the British Leyland team turned up.

On the ball

Hand-written notice on the rear window of a car in Woodstock: 'So you think I'm a bad driver. You should see me putt.'

The Los Angeles Rams American Football Club, keen to refurbish its image, has decided to change the name of its squad of girl cheer-leaders from the Rams Sundancers to the Embraceable Ewes.

Got the 'ump?

There is some concern in the West Country that the advertisement for the new Secretary of Somerset County

Cricket Club insists that he must be sponsored by two referees.

Six players have been dismissed by Kenya Breweries soccer team for using witchcraft. Kenneth Matiba, chairman of the Kenya Football Federation, had already this year warned clubs about witchcraft 'which has become an epidemic in football'. The six, all internationals, 'attended more to ju-ju than their own coach'.

Red Tales

Key difference
A story popular in Bonn tells of the following exchange between an East and West German. The East German: 'You know, the essential difference between you and us consists of you treasuring the money while we treasure the people.'
The West German: 'Correct. So we lock up our money and you lock up your people.'

On the beat
'Why do policemen patrol in threes?' is a question popular in Czechoslovakia. The answer: 'Because one can read, one can write – and the third is needed to keep an eye on these intellectuals.'

Still friends
A wreath laid by the Soviet 'ideologist', Boris Ponomarev, on Karl Marx's tomb in Highgate cemetery bore a suitably sober inscription. . . . In less formal vein was an anonymously inscribed bouquet alongside: 'Thanks for the help, Karl.'

From Prague comes the story of the foreman in charge of building a new river bridge who was asked if he had any ideas about how its load-bearing capacity should be tested. 'I think we should get fifty lorry loads of Russian troops to drive across it', he said. 'If it holds, we'll know it's a good bridge, and if it doesn't, even better.'

Farmer's tale
A very Russian definition of the word 'slander' is given in the tale of a group of Western correspondents, mis-

directed to a run-of-the-mill collective farm instead of the usual show-place for foreign visitors. 'What can we show them?' worried members of the collective asked their chairman.

'Take them to the barn', he says. 'But you know the barn has a big hole in the roof and it lets in the rain', they protest.

'Never mind', he replies. 'Then take them to the pig-sties.' 'But they haven't been mucked out for a year.'

'After that you can take them out into the fields.' 'But we didn't plough this year and the weeds are shoulder high. These correspondents will go home and tell the West that Soviet collective farming is in terrible shape.'

'If they want to go back and slander us, that's their affair,' states the chairman.

Managing the news

According to a joke doing the rounds in Prague, a Czecho-slovakian Skoda car was well trounced by a British Mini in a race.

English newspapers reported that the Mini won convincingly. Pravda, which also picked up the story, said the Skoda had finished second and the Mini one from last.

Necessary question

Graffito in a Crouch End pub: 'Is Marx's grave a Communist plot?'

Holiday Snaps

Fabulous

'Why not treat yourself to a fabulous, get-away-from-it-all weekend?' asks an advertisement in a South London newspaper. 'An unforgettable weekend is laid on for you, starting with British Rail travel, 2nd class . . .'

Sang-froid

A car seen on the Cherbourg ferry had a hand-printed notice in the rear window: 'Je conduis à droite pour le premier fois. Pardonnez des errors. SVP.' Next to this was a Blood Transfusion Service sticker: 'Give Blood.'

Even in these tourist-ridden days, a Surrey reader tells me she was mildly surprised in Canterbury to find herself and her husband accosted by a fellow Briton with the words: *'Excuse me, do you understand English?'*

Never too late
The February issue of Pan Am's Clipper Magazine includes the useful advice that 'with few exceptions tickets are always available at London theatre box offices on the day of performance or soon thereafter'.

Oh, Mr Porter
An elderly woman passenger at Manchester Airport who confided to a receptionist that she was making her first flight and asked why the departure had been delayed, was told: 'There is a crew change, Madam.'

She turned to her husband and said: 'There you are, dear. We change at Crewe.'

A free week's holiday by narrow boat from Oxford had no takers, the owners tell me, though it was worth £112 and offered simply because of a sudden cancellation. But forty-six people telephoned to ask what the catch was.

Natural assumption
Among details requested in a questionnaire sent to applicants for holiday accomodation in a Norfolk chalet camp is: Number of children (by sex). One answer read: 'Three (and one by adoption)'.

Small world
Heard from a middle-aged American woman in a Kensington hotel bar: 'What really hurt Joe was that when we booked in here the manager had never even heard of him. Back home in Winnetka, he's world famous.'

A reader, relieved to be safe back from holiday, reports having seen this chilling sign in Oxfordshire: 'Lower Hades Road. Cul de sac.'

Not the ticket
There was relief at this year's Plymouth Navy Day that visitors by car seemed actually to have come for the right reason. Last year, one driver complained that she had paid £1 at Devonport Dockyard gate and was still waiting an hour later to cross the Tamar Bridge.

Better safe
Observed in the Terminal 2 departure lounge at Heathrow

Airport was an Arab in traditional dress, surrounded by his large family. He was busily engaged in cutting the labels off Marks and Spencer garments.

A reader recently in New York spotted the sign, 'English dollars gladly exchanged', in a souvenir shop window and entered to point out the mistake. The jovial proprietor thanked her profusely for being so observant. Later, while she was paying for a Statue of Liberty model, he confided to her that 'Britishers' who came in to correct the error were responsible for more than twenty per cent of his trade during the tourist season.

Chips galore
An American who is touring Britain by car was quite overcome by the Cotswold country, but was astonished by the number of villages with exactly the same name. 'After Chipping Sodbury', he said, 'there were three villages in a row named Loose Chippings'.

Priorities
In the courtyard at Warwick Castle there is a signboard proclaiming:

ARMOURY
DUNGEON
TORTURE CHAMBER
GIFT SHOP.

One visitor's comment was: 'Ah, the ultimate horror!'

Workaday (or Two) Britain

Dividing lines
A notice in a Hampshire baker's shop: 'There are only two good unions. The Mothers' Union and Rugby Union.'

I swear to tell . . .
In proceedings to restore his name to the ballot paper in an election for a key post in the building trades' union, UCATT, Ivor Jordan told a High Court judge: 'The objection was that during the working week I would not be residing within striking distance of head office.'

He won his case.

The Industrial Society tells me that it had to cancel its Jubilee conference on 'Successful Britain' because only three people said they wanted to attend.

Striking comment
Chalked on the back of a petrol tanker on the M1: 'Going slow. Please pass.'

Exclusive
'Gala Dance, Saturday. . . . Union members and guests only', proclaims a poster in a Birmingham staff canteen. On it someone has added: 'This is a closed hop.'

My colleagues in Manchester tell me that a new word has been coined on the Northern industrial scene to describe the apparent death wish of some groups of worker;. They call it Merseycide.

Out but in
I am delighted by the comment of a leader of a walk-out in the Navy Department at Bath: 'If members cannot get in to work tomorrow because of the weather we may have to postpone the walk-out.'

Vulnerable
One Yorkshireman's comment on the defeat of Arthur Scargill, the miners' leader, over local productivity payments for his men was: 'If you stand between the pig and t' trough, you get your legs bitten.'

Opera-goers are still finding themselves involved in an industrial dispute – that involves no striking. A note handed out before the English National's production of Il Trovatore *regrets that 'owing to contractural problems with Equity the chorus in Act II will be without anvils'.*

Equals
From a NALGO branch magazine: 'Staff in the Homeless Families Unit withdrew the standby service in April to further their claim for parity with payments received by social workers. As it happens, the social workers are receiving nothing for standby duties at the moment as they are taking action on this issue themselves.'

Tailpiece
Notice chalked on the back of a lorry in the Cromwell Road, west London: 'Please pass. Driver on overtime.'

*The bread strike had its own special flavour in Mayfair
yesterday. Customers at one of the area's main grocers
learned that an Arab had bought its entire supply of bread and
rolls in an early morning call, plus all its packets of yeast and
36lb of flour.*

Honest as the day . . .
Heard in a Manchester hotel bar: 'I know there are still
people who do an honest day's work. What worries me is
that most of them want a week's wages for it.'

Time and motion study
The long delays in completing the Ince 'B' power station
in Cheshire have given birth to a wide variety of site jokes.
Favourite at the moment is the foreman asking a worker
why he had just crushed a snail with his boot. The answer:
'Because it has been following me around all day.'

Et tu, Jacques?
Graffito seen at a south-coast port: 'French dockers rule –
au quai?'

Free enterprise
A poster outside an Essex church states: 'In six days the
Lord made heaven and earth, the sea and all that in them
is.' Chalked below it says: 'He was self-employed.'

*Michael Grylls, MP for North-West Surrey, tells me that
last week in the Strangers' Restaurant in the Commons he
found himself being served – and very efficiently – by a
temporary wine-waiter who turned out to be a Westminster
dustman on strike.*

Escape route
One solution to rubbish strike problems comes from a
reader who was in the United States a few years ago when
a similar problem arose.

His attorney, living in Westchester, used to gift-wrap
the day's garbage in a cardboard box, complete with red
ribbon, and put it on the back seat of his Cadillac with the
doors left unlocked.

After an average twenty-five minutes the refuse was
collected, after which he put his car away in the garage for
the night.

Irish Stories

Proof positive
Sir Patrick Macrory, former secretary of Unilever who produced the Macrory Report on local government in Northern Ireland in 1970 was speaking as an Ulsterman – as well as captain – at Walton Heath Golf Club dinner at the week-end.

He told of an Irishman who was driving back to his Antrim farm late one night when he was stopped by the police and asked if he could identify himself.

The farmer looked full square into his rear-view mirror. 'That's me', he said.

While you wait
From a Cork parish magazine: 'Murphy, furrier and taxidermist. Customers' own skins dried and dressed.'

Irish statistic
From the journal of the Federation of Sub-Postmasters: '. . . nearly half of Northern Ireland's sub-postmistresses are women'.

Slight slip
I am indebted to the Greater Manchester Police newsletter for a story about an Irishman who recently made an anonymous hoax call to the police about a bomb in a large store.

Suspecting that the call was a hoax, the officer on duty treated it with the appropriate degree of coolness, whereupon the Irishman became enraged and said he wished to complain about the policeman's attitude.

The Irishman was then asked for his name so that the complaint could be passed on – and gave it.

Not missing a thing
A visitor to Belfast noticed a gable-end inscription proclaiming: 'No Pope here.' Underneath someone had added: 'Lucky old Pope.'

From tomorrow's Telefis Eireann programmes: '6.01pm, Hell (religious documentary)'.

Only in Ireland
Shamefaced Ulster postal officials were forced to explain yesterday why the names in their telephone directory's

'alphabetical list of subscribers' begin with the firm O'Kane, P and Company.

'Well you see', explained a spokesman, confusingly, 'it was a wrong input to the computer. The girl fed in the figure nought instead of the letter "O" – I'm so sorry, I mean she fed in the letter "O" instead of the figure nought.

'Over here, figures come before letters of the alphabet, if you see what I mean . . .'

Good Lord!

Let's hope it does . . .
A notice outside a church in Beckenham reads: 'Prayer, the only commodity that isn't going up.'

A notice board at Church House, Westminster, has been carrying the injunction, 'Work for God', with a scrawl underneath saying, 'The fringe benefits are out of this world'.

Switched on
Written on a poster outside a Hampshire church: 'No connection with the Post Office. Two collections every Sunday.'

Sign outside a Southport church: 'Pray now – and avoid the Christmas rush.'

Bedtime story
A group of clergy touring Australia were accommodated in one town in a girls' school, empty because of holidays. They found in their dormitory a notice: 'If you require a mistress during the night, press the bell.'

From the properties for sale column of a Cornish newspaper I have been sent this advertisement: 'Chapel, suitable for conversion. All main services.'

Physician . . .
Notice read from the pulpit of a church in Sheffield: 'The healing service to be held next Sunday will be taken by myself. The healer, who was to have come, has gone into hospital for an operation.'

Asked whether the Church considered it a sin for a family to have two cars and a boat, a Herefordshire vicar replied this week: 'It all depends where they are parked on Sunday morning.'

No guidance
A customer in a famous London bookshop asked an assistant where she could find a particular book on theology. The assistant shook his head sadly. 'When it comes to theology', he said, 'you've just got to trust to luck'.

Revised version
A notice in a Cheshire church porch reads: 'There will be a prayer meeting in the new Church Hall on Friday, May 25, 7pm. This will be followed by coffee and sandwiches.' To this someone has added: 'Come to pray and remain to scoff.'

Mind that Language!

Watch it, vieux mate!
Painters now busy on Westminster Bridge have put up a notice at the favourite spot from which tourists photograph Big Ben. It says: 'Le paint est wet.'

Unbearable
Sign in the foyer of an Istanbul hotel: 'Ladies are requested not to have children in the cocktail lounge.'

The hazards of translation are revealed by the recent banning of 'Upstairs, Downstairs', the TV series, in Argentina – after just one episode. Apparently the censor took great exception to the overtones of class warfare in the title, which emerged into Spanish as, 'Los de arriba, los de abajo', literally, 'Masters and underdogs'.

Soot in the eye
At Manchester airport there is a rule that only urgent calls for passengers should be given over the public address system. A recent appeal 'for the person meeting three unaccompanied minors' brought a prompt complaint that National Coal Board employees were being given preferential treatment.

End of bliss
A visitor to Italy who prided herself on her efforts to learn
the language was the only member of a party of tourists
able to read a notice on the staircase of a Naples monument.
It said: 'This staircase is in a dangerous condition. It will
be closed at the end of the tourist season.'

Heavenly
When the steward on a recent British Caledonian trans-
atlantic flight announced that 'high tea' would be served,
an American passenger inquired if that term was used
because of the altitude at which they were flying.

*A recent visitor to Peking tells me that the literal re-
translation from Chinese for parking meter is 'steel, coin-
eating tiger'.*

Love's brief chord
Miriam Makeba, the intriguing South African singer, has
had a new record album issued in Paris under the title,
'Comme une symphonie d'amour'. The first track is
'Malaisha', which I am told when translated from Xhosa
into English reads: 'Bring the axe.'

Family likeness
Sir Patrick Macrory, the military historian, sent me this
story about the late Sir Gerald Templer during his days in
Malaya. Templer wanted to rebuke some villagers for
weak behaviour towards the Communist insurgents. He
addressed them in blunt, soldierly terms, but, of course
his words had to be translated:
    Templer (in English): You're a pack of useless bastards!
    Translation: The General says he knows none of your
fathers and mothers were married to each other.
    Templer: I'll show you I can be an even bigger bastard!
    Translation: But the General says his father and mother
were not married either.
    Mind you, he won in the end; but not with words.

Blazing row
From a hotel bedroom in Grasse in the south of France:
'If you hear the alarm, quickly leave the room, shut the
door, and go downstairs without losing your temper.'

*After two years in Britain the scion of a very rich Chinese
family now realises why his experience on arrival makes
English friends laugh. Speaking very little English, he was*

21

asked repeatedly by an immigration officer 'Have you got any money?' Understanding at last, the visitor leaned over and whispered confidentially: 'How much do you want?'

End of the line
An American liaison officer attached to a British Army unit near London wished to telephone another Unit HQ. After considerable delay, the operator reported: 'You are through now, sir', to which the (by then) irate American replied: 'I've not even spoken to them yet!'

Communication gap
'Start your own language school. Very lucrative business. Knowledge of languages not necessary.' – from the current issue of *India Weekly*.

Grave Matters

Outlook gloomy
'Accommodation for the Aged: Grave Shortage' – headline in a Shropshire newspaper.

One careful owner?
An advertisement in a West Bridgford, Nottingham, sub-post office reads: 'For sale. Second-hand tombstone. Bargain for family named Perkin.'

Unlucky dip
The gloom of the Stock Exchange was slightly alleviated yesterday by this story:

Holders of European Ferries shares are entitled to subsidised journeys on the company's cross-Channel ferries, while share owners in Dundonian (formerly the Dundee Crematorium Company) are entitled to free cremation. It follows, therefore, that if any individual holds shares in both he can get buried at sea for next to nothing.

Or necessary?
'Manager required for funeral service. No living accommodation available.' – from a local newspaper.

It's good to know
From a Lincolnshire local paper: 'The Chief Fire Officer has inspected Boston Crematorium and reported to the Amenity Committee that all escape routes are adequate.'

A spokesman for the striking undertakers interviewed on Capital Radio said of the dispute: 'It's very unfortunate, but we are fighting for a living wage.'

From the Mouths of . . .

1,001 passengers
A four-year-old girl watching an incoming plane load of turbanned Indians at Heathrow airport was heard to exclaim: 'What are all these genies doing here?'

The first Noel
A seven-year-old girl taken to her brother's end-of-term carol concert at his school in Wigtownshire was given 5p to put into the collection plate. 'Do we have to pay for this?' she demanded indignantly.

From Wiltshire I am sent the story of a five-year-old boy who saw a rainbow for the first time, stared at it suspiciously, and demanded to know what it was a commercial for.

One downmanship
The six-year-old niece of a Cheltenham reader announced proudly to her friends: 'My granny's dying.' To which a boy retorted: 'That's nothing! My grandpa's already dead!'

Ready for the off
A writer in the *Church Times* tells of a small boy who sat by his father during a long and boring sermon. Spotting the red glow of a sanctuary lamp in a side chapel, he whispered to his father: 'When the light turns green, can we go?'

Card in a Southampton shop window: 'Schoolboy wishes to change knitted Christmas tie and gloves for white mice or anything else useful.'

Office routine
Describing the modern decor of her father's office in a school essay, a pupil referred to there being 'a lot of rough mating on the floor'.

Killing two birds . . .
'Dear Grandma, it was awful of me not to write and thank you before now for the £1 you sent me at Easter. It would serve me right if you forgot my birthday on May 28.' – from a letter received by a Shropshire reader from her grandson.

Heard from a small Lancashire girl outside Buckingham Palace: 'We haven't got a name on our front gate either!'

Thanks
Old Radnor parish magazine reports that a small boy was asked if he said his prayers at night. 'No, mother does it for me', he replied. 'She says, "Thank God you're in bed at last" '.

Officialdumb

Whitehall

Secrets by the ton
There was great consternation at the Ministry of Defence over the publication in this newspaper of the tonnage of the Royal Navy's planned new diesel-electric submarine. Our Naval Correspondent was accused of revealing an official secret.

'But you gave the figures', he protested.

'That was in metric tonnes', they replied, 'which is not secret.'

To get the real figure from the metric figure it is necessary – well, useful – to have a conversion table and a pocket calculator. It is fortunate the Russians do not have these, Mr Bond, or it would be the end of civilisation as we know it today . . .

An official who inquired of the Civil Service Department about the number of women of Under-Secretary rank and above was told the answer was 23½. The half-woman, apparently, was holding a temporary appointment.

Red tape rules
Before Vice-Admiral Sir Ian McIntosh, chairman of the Trust which is to run the Navy's last war-time destroyer

Cavalier as a museum at Southampton, could go ahead with arrangements for the ship to be towed from Chatham on her final voyage he had to ask for a permit from the Home Office.

Because all her guns are still in working order he had to buy a fire-arms certificate.

Counting pennies

According to the Department of Transport, the cost of the recently opened Lewes by-pass amounted to £4,851,653 and 90 pence.

Local authorities

Simple as ABC

The Kent County Council Staff Vacancy Circular No 22/79 advertises for 'Library Assistants: Dartford Division: Would suit school leaver who enjoys meeting the public. Wide variety of duties including working with books.'

Bath Council is currently advertising for a grave-digger under supervision of their Department of Leisure and Tourist Services.

Passing the buck

A curious story is related in the latest issue of the West Yorkshire police newspaper, *West Yorkshireman*, of the police officer who rang a local council to make arrangements for the disposal of a dog killed in a road accident.

If the dog was on the footpath, the council official explained, the Parks and Amenities Department dealt with it, but on the road it was a Highways Department responsibility.

No, said the officer, it was at the police station. 'Ah, well, in that case', said the official, 'it comes under Environmental Health.'

Later that morning the dog was collected by the Cleansing Department.

Havering Council, I hear, is having trouble filling the post of emergency planning officer to maintain life there after a nuclear explosion, to carry out evacuation procedures in the event of floods, and to 'marshal public safety against unexploded bombs, terrorist attacks and hi-jacking'. The job, which carries a salary of more than £4,000, is reassuringly described as 'part-time'.

One in the eye
The local council at Barnsley, South Yorkshire, has had to abandon a civil defence command post designed to survive a nuclear war because it has been wrecked by vandals.

City Corporation planning department, shown photographs of London's highest office block, the Natwest Tower, protested that no planning permission had been given for statues on the topmost storey. Then it was discovered the figures weren't statues, they were workers.

Common Market

Not a prayer
Farmers' scepticism about the benefits of the Common Market can only have been reinforced by the tit-bit of information given at a recent Sussex farmers' dinner.

There are, remarked the speaker, 56 words in the Lords' Prayer, 297 in the Ten Commandments, 300 in the American Declaration of Independence, and 26,911 in an EEC directive on the export of duck eggs.

Pooh to you
The final bulletin of the last non-elected European Parliament concludes the summary of its recent Luxembourg session as follows:

'The House also discussed Mr Shaw's reports on company audits and budget carry-overs, Mr Kaspereit's reports on Cyprus grapes . . . Mr Jahn's report on environmental carcinogens, Mr van der Gun's report on Winnie the Pooh . . .'

Winnie der who? . . . Please relax! Anxious inquiries uncover this story. The committeeman from Holland had a highly esoteric report, written in sociologist terms, about promotion of education contacts between European colleges.

'What shall we title it?' No-one could think of anything under a sociological paragraph in length. Silence descended until a voice at the back cried: 'Oh, call it Winnie the Pooh.' And they did.

A good pennyworth
A competition to recruit new staff has been announced by the General Secretariat of the Council of the European Communities. Applicants are being issued a four-

page form. Apart from personal details, with parents' address and next of kin, and a photograph, it also asks for full details of education, including post-graduate studies, works published ('indicate particularly works connected with the post applied for') and languages spoken.

The jobs available are for seven store-hands and a cloak-room attendant. The latter, however, is open to applicants of both sexes so perhaps some skills above the ordinary may be necessary.

And everywhere

That'll teach 'em
A reader just back from Lagos tells me that the new Nigerian constitution, to which the final touches are now being put, includes a decree that makes *coups d'état* illegal.

South African insistence on bi-lingual signs means that minor road junctions carry the warning 'Stop Stop' – the first command being in English, the second in Afrikaans.

Targets of the mob
Ayatollah Khomeini's men have many ways of condemning supporters of the Shah's reign in Iran. An American woman, married to a rich Iranian, has just received a letter warning her against trying to return to Teheran.

It seems that when the revolutionaries ransacked her house they 'discovered' in the basement not only a wine cellar, which is bad enough, but also a 'torture room' – a small, windowless, wood-lined room with spartan furniture.

We would call it a sauna.

Catch ni-ni
Journalists arriving at the Tokyo buildings where the seven-nation economic 'summit' meeting is to be held were stopped by armed police who said they could not go inside without a special pass. Asked where these passes could be obtained, the police replied: 'Inside . . .'

Very civil servant
Sign at the entrance to a tax collector's office, reported by a holidaymaker from Florida: 'Sorry folks, we're open.'

Oh, Dear Me!

Test your strength
A notice at Kent University in Canterbury proclaims: 'Unused chest expander for sale – cannot get the lid off the box.'

Graffito seen in a Covent Garden wine bar: 'Apathy ru   '

Another inscription from the same wine bar: 'I used to be indecisive but now I'm not so sure.'

Reverse thrust
Seen on a Brighton–Portsmouth train: 'Dyslexia rules – KO.'

Distance lends . . .
Heard from an American woman at Stonehenge: 'It *must* be wonderful, Bertha – we've come so far!'

Blessed relief
A notice at a Bridport, Dorset, church states: 'The meek shall inherit the earth.' To which someone has added: 'If that's all right with you.'

Board and Lodging

Shore thing
From a brochure issued by an Essex hotel: 'This is a comfortable and friendly family hotel in a superb position on the promenade. Children love it because, unlike some resorts, the sea comes right up to the shore.'

Sea it all
Seaford's town guide boasts: 'We have all the sea you could possibly want. Miles and miles of it stretch to the horizon.'

Early warning
From a commercial travellers' hotel guide just received: '. . . Electric blankets in each bed. Live entertainment. Wed, Sat.'

Bedtime story
A Winchester priest came to London for an ecclesiastical gathering at which he was to take part in a service. Booking into an hotel which could offer him only a double room, he was delighted to find when he went to bed that his pyjamas had been laid out on one pillow and his lace-edged cotta neatly on the other.

Demarcation line
Sign in a Dover restaurant: 'We have an agreement with the Bank of England. They don't sell food and we don't cash cheques.'

Staff efficiency in hotels takes different forms. British businessmen in Peking have discovered that a request for a morning alarm call to the switchboard at the Friendship Hotel results in the operator ringing and peremptorily telling sleepy guests: 'Get up!' She continues to repeat the order until satisfied that it is being obeyed.

Warm welcome
A friend just back from New York tells me he walked into a hotel in Manhattan to be greeted by this notice: 'Attack-trained Dobermans loose in the lobby.'

Bread and circuses
Included among the heated swimming pools, stables, saunas and other attractions offered by hotels and guest houses in a current family holiday brochure is the down-to-earth appetizer from Southport: 'Free crusts for ducks in park.'

Don't call us
A Briton recently returned from Kano, northern Nigeria, sends me a notice from an hotel there which is most refreshing in its honesty: 'Orders for meals, snacks or drinks through room service will take a minimum of delay. Guests who require fast service are requested to use our dining room or the bar.'

When the new barman in a Buckinghamshire pub was asked if he had any half Coronas he puzzled a moment, then said brightly: 'Orange or lemonade, sir?'

Easy
Sign in an Istanbul hotel room: 'To call room service please open door and call Room Service.'

Travellers' Tales

Of public woe . . .

Waiting for it
Seen in a New York subway station: 'Gloria Mundi is sic of the transit.'

Not worth the paper
A woman haughtily refused to accept one of the new time-tables being handed out at a South London railway station yesterday with the words: 'You must be joking! You need that more than we do.'

This announcement was made by the guard on Monday's London–Berwick express train: 'Good morning, ladies and gentlemen. This is the nine o'clock train for Berwick, calling at Peterborough, York, Darlington, Newcastle and Berwick. May God bless and be with you.'

Better than the Post
Asked by a colleague when the next bus was due, a rather doleful inspector at Waterloo replied: 'We don't have a timetable any more. We only guarantee same day delivery.'

The state of London's underground carriages is sadly all too familiar to many. But a reader received quite a shock yesterday when, on the Wimbledon to Edgware Road train, in car No 22609, he saw a spider with enough confidence to begin weaving a web.

I now hear of a pigeon that regularly likes to hop into trains at Edgware Road station, have a peck around, and then alight at Paddington.

No go
An announcement heard over Southern Region Waterloo loud speakers: 'There is no toilet accommodation on the Alton part of the train. We apologise for the inconvenience.

A reader arrived at Charing Cross to find that the 7.58am fast train had been cancelled and was told by the station officer to take the 8.20am instead. 'Isn't that a slow train?' she asked. 'Not slow', said the Indian on duty, 'just semi-fast'.

If you can't beat 'em . . .
Notice reported from Chelmsford station: 'Proposed fare increases. Why not join us? Vacancies exist for booking clerks at this station . . .'

And private grief

Basic knowledge
'If a traffic signal changes to amber only', a Norfolk driving instructor asked a young woman L-driver, 'what will you see next?'

Her unhesitating reply was: 'Some fool man trying to beat the lights.'

From the Anglo-Japanese Economic Institute I learn that an explosion a minute is being used by police to stop drivers falling asleep on one monotonous stretch of road in Japan.

Highway halt
Notice outside a church in California: 'Last chance to pray before the freeway.'

When pupils at a Sussex school were asked to 'write not more than fifty words on what you would do to encourage motorists to show more consideration for others', one twelve-year-old had the short answer: 'Drive a police car.'

Acceptable face . . .?
'Lada Estate . . . 1,400 miles . . . owner getting company car' – from the *Morning Star*'s classified advertisements.

Fail-safe
A successful move is reported from Pennsylvania to get motorists to slow down on a stretch of road there. Three words on a newly erected sign have done the trick: 'Caution – Nudists crossing.'

It is not often that drivers need hospital treatment after an accident in which their cars did not even touch. In Gutersloh, Germany, recently, two drivers approaching each other in fog were craning out of their windows trying to see the white line. They banged their heads together.

Sunday driver?
I have been sent a cutting from the *Richmond and Twicken-ham Times* of a letter complaining about the traffic in Petersham. The writer concludes: 'I erected a small sign

by my shattered fences saying "God preserve me from incompetent drivers." A passing vicar ran over it!'

Highway warning
Sign on a main road in America: 'Last year in this State gas killed 421 people. Seven inhaled it, 14 put a match to it and 400 stepped on it.'

Person-alities

Already?
A middle-aged gentleman on a bus in Kensington High Street, offering his seat to a lady, apologised: 'I am afraid this is illegal.'

Heard in a pub: 'So I said to my wife that I didn't mind being ruled constitutionally by a woman – or even politically – but I drew the line at domestically.'

Toofer the price
Employers have come up with a new solution to the many and furious accusations of discrimination that are bandied about within the United States. Personnel departments are told always to try and hire a 'toofer'.

This new being is black and female and is reckoned as two-for-the-price-of-one. Afterwards you may be accused of many things – but not discrimination.

As expected
Inscribed, I am told, on the wall of the ladies' loo at the Equal Opportunities Commission are the words: 'When God created man, She was only joking.'

An oil sheikh takeover is one thing, observes a reader, but does a local newspaper report of a bride with 'a bouquet of harem lilies' mean that monogamy itself is now to be superseded?

Keeping a balance
To a slogan on the wall of a South London station, 'God was a woman', a chauvinist has added: 'Until She changed Her mind.'

Unisexism

A Philadelphia group calling itself the High School Women's Collective is to sponsor a discussion next month on 'Sexism in the Municipal Schools'. The discussion is open to girls only.

In its quest for 'religious absurdities' a new weekly, the Christian World, *discovered a new rendering by an American group of Whittier's hymn 'Dear Lord and Father of Mankind'. This now runs, 'Dear Mother-Father of Personkind'. Fortunately the second line, 'Forgive our foolish ways', is left untouched.*

Unkindest cut

An understandably aggrieved colleague insists she overheard a man saying to his wife outside a jeweller's shop in Fleet Street: 'Darling, I think I'll have your ears pierced.'

Strolling through the Westminster Hall exhibition marking the fiftieth anniversary of women's suffrage, Anne Warren, wife of the Tory MP for Hastings, noticed an error over historical dates. When she drew it to a woman official's attention, she was a bit taken aback to be told it would be 'referred to the man in charge'.

Almost unisex

Seen in a Brighton employment bureau window: 'Tealady wanted urgently – either sex.'

Lesser breed

Card spotted in a South Kensington shop window: 'Charlady seeks charwoman to take over her duties while she is on holiday.'

Eco-Soundings

Warm words

Scrawled on a wall in North London: 'Save oil, burn tourists.'

T-bone steaks may one day be occupying the attention of the Department of Health doomsday people. A Maryland nutritionist, Dr Lon Crosby, has estimated that a person who eats two 12oz charcoal-broiled steaks a week gets more tar than he would from smoking two packets of cigarettes a day.

Covering the field
Stickers seen on an East Sussex Landrover – on the windscreen, 'Southdown Hunt' and on the rear window, 'Help preserve endangered wild life.'

Stop whaling
Garrard's, the Crown jewellers, who recently have been advertising their sumptuous Christmas items, received an angry letter from an animal preservationist who objected to their whalebone candle-snuffer. This, he complained, was an unnecessary burden to place on an animal facing extinction.

They replied with truly regal disdain: 'Although we understand your concern with the preservation of the whale, the whalebone that we use comes only from dead whales . . .'

A car-bumper sticker seen in Phoenix, Arizona: 'You lost your job and you're hungry? Eat an environmentalist.'

Beyond all hope
Pupils at a Camberwell school were asked to write not more than fifty words about the harmful effect of oil on sea life. One eleven-year-old wrote: 'When my mum opened a tin of sardines last night it was full of oil and all the sardines were dead.'

Eerie
The Royal Society for the Protection of Birds is having to produce its film about osprey's nesting habits at least a year late. A hide was built in Scotland and the cameraman, Hugh Miles, waited patiently. But when they arrived, the ospreys decided to build a new eyrie – right on top of the hide.

Well Named

Up the spout
Among recent runners at Lingfield Park races was Tea Pot. The jockey was M. Kettle. Punters who backed a cosy win, alas, got only the dregs.

34

With the arrival of a new cashier at a branch of Barclays Bank in Leicestershire, a Miss K. Swindell now works alongside Miss J. E. Crooks.

Promises, promises
The burnt-down synagogue in Archway Road, Highgate, is being rebuilt. The large signboard outside gives the name of the builder as Solomon.

That respected Roman Catholic journal, The Clergy Review, *is thinking of changing its name to* The Catholic Review *to make it clear it serves non-clerics, too. A slightly different name problem affected its stable-companion,* The Tablet, *back in the sixties – some people took it to be a journal designed to advise Catholics about the pill.*

Right royal
The current fad of printing the names of the occupants of a car at the top of the windscreen reached a peak of one-upmanship, surely, with this announcement seen in Southampton: 'My husband and I'.

My story of the Australian who could not find the tomb of Marks and Spencer in Highgate cemetery reminded a Cumbrian reader of two women inspecting the churchyard at Grasmere. After a thorough search they expressed disappointment at not being able to find Woolworth's grave.

Clerical error
In New York, the bishops of both dioceses, Albany and Buffalo, shared the Christian name, William. In a letter to his colleague, the Bishop of Albany followed the normal practice of writing his diocese as his surname and signed himself William Albany. His neighbour, however, signed his reply 'Buffalo Bill'.

Staff at a poultry firm in Haverfordwest must have been in two minds about entering its recent beauty contest. The winner, twenty-year-old Christine Morgan, has to spend the next year trying to live down – or, indeed, live up to – the title of Miss Wonderbreast.

Every wheel counts
After saying he was 'transport manager' at Tesco's, a South Humberside man was asked what he had to do in such a highly responsible job. 'Look after the trollies in the shop', was the reply.

By another name . . .
A man who applied for a job in the West Country described his last position as 'Room Director'. Inquiries revealed he had been a bouncer at a London club.

The owner of a new bookmaker's shop in Dawlish, South Devon, is a Mr Gamble. 'Something I've always wanted to do', says Mr Gamble, a bank clerk until recently.

Name dropping
According to the Hong Kong Tourist Association, the Crown Colony boasts some remarkably apt shop names, including the Hang On Medicine Co., the Lee Kee Boot and Shoemaker Ltd., the Hop On Bicycle Shop and the Wing King Optical Ltd.

There is also a popular Hong Kong TV personality, Ivan Ho.

Ill Written

Amazing discovery
From the National Economic Development Committee's report on the food and drink industries: 'Total food demand tends to be constrained by the size of the human stomach.'

A Hampshire council noticeboard reads: 'Household Waste Amenity Point'. A local resident has translated it, correctly: 'Rubbish Tip'.

Writ small
Dr Mervyn Stockwood, Bishop of Southwark . . . provides an extract from a book by Bruce Reed called *The Dynamics of Religion*, which the Diocesan Bishops of the Church of England were required to discuss at a meeting in Salisbury.

Reed defines the primary task of the local church as follows:

'To monitor the oscillation process by containing or rendering manageable anxieties associated with the activities of the profane world so that individuals and institutions are able to carry out the tasks on which the survival and well-being of their social groups depends.'

Doctors worried that drink can cause brain damage were reported yesterday to have organised a symposium to air their views. The Oxford and Chambers' dictionaries agree that the primary definition of 'symposium' is a 'drinking party'.

Decisions, decisions
Minute No 5 for the next meeting of the Torbay Sports Advisory Council executive committee . . . reads: 'To appoint a sub-committee to investigate ways and means of setting up proposed sub-committees.'

They don't leave much to the imagination in the City. An eminent firm of stockbrokers has issued a prospectus to potential shareholders in a fleet of helium and hot-air powered airships. One section explains: 'Casualties in aviation are generally caused by involuntary vertical movement towards the ground.'

High-pitched wine .
It is good to see readers so quick to pounce on pompous nonsense such as this description of a French wine:

'The name Comte de Voguë is supreme sovereign in the group of the world's red wines. When the wines of '71 produced by these vineyards have attained ten years of age, they will no longer be mere wines, but dreams, liquid grace, elixirs of the gods that one guards like jewels, and preferably drinks only at one's own funeral, for no moment of life can be so precious as to demand such a celebration.'

A new building at Portsmouth has been officially called a Passenger Transport Exchange. It is a bus station.

Woe Is Me !

The big debate
Car-sticker spotted in the Plymouth area: 'There's a place for you in the modern Royal Navy . . . mine.'

The pity of it
Mournful advertisement in *Visor*, journal of the British troops in Northern Ireland 'For sale. Double bed 6ft 7in × 5ft. Less than one year old. Only half used . . .'

Another engagement
From *Railway Magazine*: 'Enthusiast, getting married, everything must go, complete collection of signs, nameplates, lamps, magazines, paperwork and much more . . .' Much more, indeed!

Overheard in a City office: 'Not only does this firm give you a pension, but working here will age you more quickly.'

Weighty matters
Overhead in a greengrocer's shop in Totnes: 'I would like 3lb of potatoes, please, but could I have all small ones because the big ones are so heavy to carry.'

Such suffering
In a Bloomsbury café, a barefoot, bearded youth in tattered jeans was heard to remark disconsolately: 'I'm squatting in Chelsea at the moment but I'll have to move out. There isn't enough space for my stereo equipment.'

Pennyworth
Overheard in Harrow during conversation between two housewife shoppers: 'A 10p doesn't buy anything any more. I call them tennies.'

Revised version
Latest car sticker seen in Portsmouth: 'Will the last man leaving the Navy please close the dockyard gates.'

Love and Marriage

Buzz off
'What is cross-pollination?' asks a question in a general knowledge test for pupils at a Surrey school. A twelve-year-old girl answered: 'This is when the female flower is not in the mood.'

Ultimate sanction
Overheard from a young woman speaking of her boyfriend in a Manchester restaurant: 'I wish that I was married to him so that I could divorce him!'

Brief encounter
Seen outside a Birmingham cinema: 'Love is a Many Splendoured Thing – for three days only.'

A pharmacy in the Chinese city of Tientsin started distributing contraceptives free of charge but found that many people were too embarrassed to ask for them. My correspondent in Peking says the problem could have been because of the four sizes available: large, medium, small, and a final category which translates as 'extra small' or 'miniature'. A self-service take-away has been opened.

Voice control
Heard from a girl in a Manchester café: 'I thought oral contraception was when you talked your way out of it.'

QED
Card in a Birmingham shop window: 'Small furnished flat or similar required by young married couple, wife out all day, husband on night work. No children.'

Heard in the main shopping centre at Seaford, Sussex: a middle-aged man, obviously a visitor, asking a woman passer-by: 'Where's Marks and Spencer, please?' Her reply that there wasn't one in the town shook him badly. 'Good heavens', he said, 'I'm supposed to be meeting my wife there'.

No connection?
Consecutive announcements over the public address system at John Lewis's, Oxford Street: 'Attention, please. Would Mrs — please go to the information desk where her husband is waiting for her.'

'Attention, please. Visitors to Oxford Street and the West End are warned to keep a close watch on their valuables.'

Wife style
Heard from a young woman in a Bradford café: 'Tom wants me to stick to cooking and cleaning and looking after the kids. He says no wife of his is going to work.'

One every day
A large store on Lagos Marina has been selling a Christmas card, neatly designed and bearing the words: 'Wishing a Happy Christmas to my adored wife.' It comes boxed in packs of twelve.

The card
While serving in Nigeria during the Second World War, a reader tells me he became friendly with a student at a Church Missionary Society college. 'We have kept up a

correspondence for the past thirty-eight years. My friend had planned to visit me this summer but unhappily died before this could be achieved. His son, my godson, wrote of his father's death which, he said, had left him with many problems.

'For example, his father had had eight wives and forty-six children! . . .'

My correspondent adds that during all those thirty-eight years he knew only of one wife and four sons. Clearly the salesmen of Lagos know their market!

From the Parish News of St Mary Magdalene Latimer with Flaunden, Buckinghamshire: '*Mothers Union – sale of unwanted items. Please bring your husbands.*'

Ah, well!
Headline in the house magazine of a Birmingham company 'Pensioners wed: fifty-year-old friendship ends at altar.'

Laura Norder

Verdict from above
David McNee, Commissioner of the Metropolitan Police, was asked whether it was true that police morale was low. He could only cite the case of the Chief Superintendent who saw one of his constables standing in Trafalgar Square, looking up at the pigeons, wiping his eye and saying: 'Go on, do it again. Everybody else does.'

Note pinned to the front door of a house on a new estate in Southampton: '*If you are thinking of burgling this place in search of money please do not hesitate to knock and ring at any time of night as I would like to help you look for it.*'

Sound choice
Sign over a display of burglar alarms in a Hampshire ironmongers: 'For the man who has everything.'

Overheard on the No 290 Alder Valley bus passing the modern Coldingley prison at Bisley: '*It's so cosy in there now that they're floodlighting it at night to stop people climbing in.*'

Taking no risks

One of our reporters at the National Front meeting in Brixton was asked the time by a policeman in the cordon around the school.

Having told the policeman the hour, my colleague observed in a friendly way: 'Surely you're the one who's supposed to be able to tell people the time.'

The policeman's reply: 'I left my watch at home in case it got broken in any violence.'

Magistrates at Cambridge have been alarmed to hear that one of the options for craft instruction at their recently opened juvenile attendance centre is 'copper beating'.

Gilding the lily

No doubt applications are flooding in to the Spitalfields Neighbourhood Law Service after their advertisement in the *Law Society Gazette* for a community lawyer to work in 'a depraved inner-city area'.

There have been so many bank raids in New York City – 126 in the past month – that when a colleague inquired why a crowd had gathered outside a bank he was told: 'I think they iust saw someone taking money in.'

Face to face

A Cheshire local paper reported last week that a mirror worth £5 had been stolen from the cloakroom of a showhouse on a new housing estate. 'Police', its report adds, 'are looking into it'.

A colleague overheard a woman at the Buckingham Palace garden party for bishops and their wives asking an attendant: 'Can you please tell me where I could leave my raincoat where it will be safe?'

About face

From the Police Federation magazine, *Police*, comes the story of a Gloucestershire detective who wanted to use a café as an observation point and introduced himself to the manager, showing his warrant card to prove his identity.

The manager scrutinised it carefully, returned it and said: 'I'm sorry, officer, I have never seen that man in here.'

An elderly lady complained to the police in Fairport, Connecticut, recently about receiving obscene telephone calls. 'How long has this been going on?' asked the policeman. 'Thirty years', she replied.

Seasonal note
A variation on an old theme: on the back of a dusty Securicor van, the finger-painted message: 'Merry Xmas to all our raiders.'

OOPS ...

Clouded crystal
The Prophetic Witness Movement International (Southampton branch) recently placed this advertisement in the *Southern Evening Echo*: 'It is regretted that the meeting convened for September 21 has been cancelled due to unforeseen circumstances.'

From the bicentennial issue of Time *magazine: 'Britain has loaned to the US for a year a copy of the Magna Carta, signed in 1215. (In like spirit, an anonymous US institution helped the British government last week to buy back Flodden Field, site of the Battle of Hastings.)'*

For east read west
The United States, with a geographical span of some 5,000 miles from the Hawaiian Islands to the most easterly tip of Maine, has many place names repeated over and over again. Thus, precision with addresses assumes considerable importance.

Philatelists have discovered this to their cost recently as the following pained little notice in the classified advertisement columns of the *Saturday Review* attests:

'We wish to apologise publicly to the 796 members of the World Stamp Collectors' Society who went to Norwalk, Connecticut, instead of to Norwalk, California, for our annual convention because of a printer's error in our invitations.'

Et tu, La Nazione?
A brief report of the fire at Bentley Priory, Stanmore, in the Florence newspaper, *La Nazione*, describes it as the

building 'from which the RAF, the British Air Force, directed the Battle of Britain against the Spitfires of the German Luftwaffe during the summer of 1940'.

From a Lymington local paper: 'Beaulieu Young Farmers' Club met . . . in the village hall when the guest speaker was Mrs —. She gave a crockery demonstration and the items produced were later eaten by the members.'

Without comment
Publishers correction: '1978 Edition of *Dod's Parliamentary Companion*. Reference to Lord Gibson's biography on page 122: for National Front read NATIONAL TRUST.'

Guaranteed authentic
Seen in a Bristol bookshop's window: 'THE TURIN SHROUD. Signed copies.'

Not a Venus in sight
A report of a Thorpe Village, Norfolk, Women's Institute meeting states: 'A competition was held for the oddest object found on the beach and the result was – 1 Mrs H—, 2 Mrs M—, 3 Mrs A—'.

Spoil-sport
From the staff magazine of a Birmingham company: 'Correction: Miss — has been appointed to act as general supervisor of Work Area Six and not (as stated in our August issue) of Work Area Sex.'

Overseas Viewpoint

Too, too divine
This is a description of an English officer, as portrayed in *Pravda* and reprinted in the army's magazine for soldiers in Ulster, *Visor*:

The English officer is a beautiful aristocrat, extremely rich and independent, a sybarite and an epicure. He has a spoilt, capricious and blasé character, loves pornographic pictures, recherché food, strong and strange drinks.

The English officer is least of all an officer. He is a rich landowner, house-owner, capitalist or merchant and only an officer incidentally. He knows nothing about the army and the army only sees him on parades and reviews. From the professional point of view he is the most ignorant officer in Europe.

His income runs into several thousands, often tens of thousands of pounds a year. The pay he receives from the Government hardly suffices to keep him in scent and gloves. English officers, especially the younger ones, do absolutely no work of any kind.

Truth dawns
Sitting on the top of a bus in Regent Street one Eastern visitor was heard saying to another: 'Do you know, it was only yesterday that I realised Father Christmas was not a Roman Catholic priest.'

Take it easy
This Brazilian definition of the British Labour Party appears in Senhor Ismael do Prado's 'Small Political Vocabulary', published by the Rio newspaper, *Journal do Brasil*:

'Labour: In its British version is the party which, believing Britain to have worked enough in past centuries to conquer an Empire that it has since lost, offers a programme of general rest for the masses.'

Older than the hills
Heard from an American woman at Stonehenge: 'The courier says it's been here since time immemorial, but I reckon it's much older than that.'

Cultural Cul-de-Sacs

Publish it not . . .
A traveller visiting the southern Israeli town of Ashkelon lately was assured that plans were going ahead for establishing what would be known as the Philistine Cultural Centre.

Corrupting influence
Apologising for the lateness of breakfast, the proprietor of a small London hotel explained that the cook had taken the day off to visit Shakespeare's birthplace at Stratford.

With obvious disgust he added: 'She had never even heard of the fellow until she met all these American tourists.'

Con biro
On the wall of the ladies at Manchester Free Trade Hall is the instruction: 'Please Wiggle Handel.' To which someone has added: 'If I do, will it wiggle bach?'

The Scottish National Orchestra's Albert Hall Prom concert performance of Nielsen's Symphony No 4, known as 'The Inextinguishable', was sponsored by the Gulf Oil Company.

Farcical choice
A party of twenty-six distinguished Soviet theatre officials is visiting London ... After being shown round the National Theatre they were asked what play they would like to see They replied at once that their first choice was the long-running comedy 'No Sex Please – We're British'.

Out of step
Heard in a London store's book department: 'Have you a copy of La Fontaine's Fables?' – 'I don't think so, madam. We don't really get much call for books on ballet.'

A reader walking through the corridors of the Franklin Roosevelt Metro in Paris at the week-end spotted a blind beggar sitting on a stool playing accordion music – on a battery-operated tape-recorder balanced on his knee.

Kosher cowboy
Much amusement was caused backstage at the Festival Hall this week after one performance by the Batsheva dance company from Israel when, on top of a pile of lost property at the artists' entrance was seen a book entitled 'Two-Gun Cohen'.

Chilling response
The annual tourist invasion of London is already under way according to actor Donald Sinden ... 'When the tourists arrive you start to notice that all the jokes with a particularly English connotation are greeted with stony silence', he told me.

'It's very disconcerting to look out into the void, while awaiting the expected reaction and just see rows of Japanese faces staring silently back at you.'

Bel canto
Overheard in a Croydon department store: 'Have you any records of Gregorian chant, please?' Assistant, after a puzzled pause: 'I don't know. Is he in a group?'

Lack of realism
Reported from the Pompeii Exhibition at Burlington House where there is a replica of a Pompeiian garden, a mother saying to her small daughter: 'No, dear, they did not have plastic gnomes in those days.'

By Hook
As the lights went up for the interval in *Peter Pan* at the London Casino at the week-end, an American with four young children leaned across to his wife and said: 'The Oedipus angle was obvious but the immoral, amoral overtones, undertones, are more difficult to grasp.'

'Breasts, like stereo speakers, are supposed to come in pairs. If, for some reason, one is missing, distortion results.' This comes, inevitably, from an ICA *playwright's puff for her lunchtime play there.*

Purpose built
Overheard from a visitor – presumably – in the queue for the Thracian treasures exhibition at the British Museum: 'What a huge building. I wonder what it was before?'

Not to be?
Spotted by a friend at the start of a road in Wallington, Surrey: One house numbered 2A and next door one named 'Hamlet'.

Hutber's Law

That's co-operation
Hutber's Law was formulated by the late Patrick Hutber while City Editor of *The Sunday Telegraph* and refined by him into three words: improvement means deterioration!

A nice example of this has just come on to my desk from a Berkshire reader. It is a note from her milkman stating: 'Kindly note that as from next Sunday there will be no

Sunday delivery. We trust you will co-operate with us to make this a success.'

A notice in a West Country hotel room assured a colleague he need no longer fear 'intrusion' on his evening privacy as the chambermaid would no longer come to turn his bed down unless special arrangements were made. The management added solemnly that it hoped guests would appreciate this new service.

Getting it right
A card in a Newcastle hotel proclaimed: 'We would like to apologise for the improvements we are making.'

From the current issue of the Grocer: *'One innovation is the use of a refined trolley to trolley check-out system. Instead of the goods being moved out of one trolley to the next by the check-out operator, this work is done by the customer.'*

Helping hand
Notice in the foyer of an hotel in the Scottish Highlands: 'For the convenience of guests, there is no bus service on Saturday and Sunday . . .'

The New York Telephone Company has just received permission to raise the price it charges subscribers for not printing their names in the telephone directory.

Cold comfort
From the current Labour manifesto for the Forest of Dean district council elections: 'Rates: This was once a problem for the rich. Because Socialism has improved our way of life it is now a problem for everybody.'

As Easy as A-B-ZEE

He should know
In the latest issue of *Professional Administration*, the official publication of the Institute of Chartered Secretaries and Administrators, the first article is headed: 'Great educational expenditure has not produced the long-awaited economic expansion.'

It is signed by C. A. Horn, PhD, MSc, BSc(Econ), LLB, MBIM, FCIS, FIWSP.

Hooked

In part of the cloak-room in the Sir John Cass School in the East End, a notice proclaims: 'These hooks are for teachers only.' Underneath someone has added: 'They may also be used for hats and coats.'

Post-mortem

Seen on the wall of a London teaching hospital: 'Old professors never die. They just lose their faculties.'

On the fencing outside a Barnes secondary school is the legend in two-foot-high letters: 'Elizabeth II rains, OK.'

Preparing for doomsday

After seeing one advertisement in the latest Careers Organisation Bulletin, James Woodhouse, Headmaster of Rugby, is wondering whether all this education is necessary. The advertisement, he told his school Speech Day audience, said: 'Wanted. Man to work on nuclear fissionable isotope molecular reactive counters and three-phase cyclotronic uranium photosynthesizers. No experience necessary.'

Good riddance

Observed by a clergyman attending a Retreat at Downside Abbey was a notice on a door leading from the boys' school there. This read: 'No exit for Boys except for Disposal or Rubbish.'

A recent examination paper in a London school posed the question: 'What is Britain's highest award for valour in war?' One reply, quoted to a parents' meeting was 'Nelson's column'.

Naturally

From the Cambridge University leaflet on procedure at the degree ceremony: 'Among the hoods worn by graduands in the Senate House are: Bachelor of Veterinary Medicine: similar to the hood for Bachelor of Medicine but with more fur.'

Primary knowledge

Blackboard notice outside a nursery school in Chislehurst, Kent: 'Today we are going to learn four-letter words.'

From Other Columns

Echo from afar
A reader who is working in Jeddah, Saudi Arabia, has sent me the following from his local paper, *The Saudi Gazette*, to show that Britain is not alone with her climatic problems:

'The weather forecast is cancelled today because of the weather. Forecasts are obtained from the airport and roads there from our office were impassable. Whether we get the weather tomorrow depends on the weather.'

But what else?
A Sussex newspaper headline: 'NUDISTS MAY GET COASTAL STRIP.'

A Wiltshire reader has sent me details of a notice in the latest issue of his parish magazine, signed by the vicar. It states: 'We are thinking of forming a branch of the Mothers' Union in the parish, so any ladies wishing to become mothers should meet me in the vestry after the service.'

That figures
Headline from the *West Wales Guardian*: 'Bus on fire – passengers alight'.

Tally-ho-ho
From the quarterly newsletter of a Devonshire equestrian club. 'Col — said he could not abide sloppiness; girls who rode to hounds should ride dressed properly or not at all.'

My tribute to the Geneva newspaper La Suisse *for the best definition yet of statistics: 'If I put my wife's head in the refrigerator and her feet in the oven, her average body temperature will be perfectly normal.'*

Late news
From a Lincolnshire school magazine: 'Old boys are requested to complete the form and return it as soon as possible. News of old boys who have died will be particularly welcomed.'

From a Sussex newspaper: 'Progress on the Buckhurst Place public conveniences has been slow because the builder is required to contain himself within the site . . .'

49

Questionable
The latest issue of *Psychic News* tells me that the Society for Psychical Research has produced a number of lectures on cassettes including Andrew Green on 'Are ghosts dying out?' and Dr Bernard Carr asking 'Is there a future in precognition?'

A Small Hitch

Drawing the line
Placard held by a teenage girl hitch-hiker standing by the roadside at Hook, Hampshire, at the week-end: 'Anywhere but Basingstoke.'

Free enterprise?
A Glasgow reader tells me that while driving in the South if England a few weeks ago he spotted a hitch-hiker carryong a notice that read, 'References exchanged'.

Great unwashed
Waiting on a slip-road of the M4 was a hitch-hiker, his hair everywhere, his clothing beyond redemption, and his worldly goods in a veteran knapsack. In his outstretched hand was a card bearing one word: 'BATH'.

Keep Fit

Expert opinion
Overheard by a colleague in St Thomas's Hospital, London, from a leading surgeon to a disgruntled patient: 'Sir, a little pain never hurt anyone.'

Mot juste
In a Carshalton hospital corridor, a sign was put up and survived for all of six hours: 'Psychiatry Department – round the bend.'

Letter from a GP in the latest issue of the medical magazine Pulse: '*At the Royal Show recently I visited a large pavilion bearing the title: "The National Health Service today". It was almost empty, had nothing of any general interest dis-*

played, no-one was in attendance, and the only sign of life was the clink of tea cups behind a door marked "Private." '

Safety measures

Question in a test set at a Lambeth school: 'Why does a surgeon wear a mask when he performs an operation?' One twelve-year-old wrote: 'So if he makes a muck of it the patient won't know who did it.'

There is no shortage of raw material, surely, for the lecture being given at lunchtime today in Charing Cross Hospital by Doctors R. A. Parkins and I. T. Gilmore. Their topic – 'Awkward Bleeders'.

Nervous laughter

The British have always been partial to the macabre joke. I am sorry if occasionally the more sensitive reader may wince, but they are part of our heritage and my post-bag usually has one example every day.

Indeed, yesterday, a North London reader told me of the patient who complained that her private hospital anaesthetist's bill was too high – '£200 just to put me to sleep!'

Said her doctor: 'No, it's to be sure you wake up again . . .'

Mixed bag

A nice example of religious tolerance in the National Health Service is provided by a note in this week's *British Medical Journal*. Two weeks ago, says a writer: 'I operated on an ardent Jehovah's Witness. I am a Roman Catholic, my assistant is a Moslem, the anaesthetist is a Jew, and the theatre Sister a Methodist from New Zealand.'

Key question

A Plymouth hospital's form specifically for pregnancy tests asks for surname, first names, age and sex. The reader who told me this comments: 'I can rarely resist the temptation to write "Yes".'

Advance warning

A Great Yarmouth dentist with a sense of humour which doubtless he hopes his patients share, has a 'Fasten your seatbelts' notice in front of his operating chair.

A celebrated Services' dentist always had this notice in his surgery: 'Pain is mind over matter. I don't mind and you don't matter.'

Rover's revenge
Outside the surgical block of Epsom District Hospital is a sign which reads: 'Caution – Guard Dogs Operating.'

Salesmanship

Disarming humour
Sign over a china figure of a small boy with one arm broken off, seen on a junk stall in a London street market: 'The Infant Nelson'.

Count your blessings
Seen in the window of a Hampshire dairy: 'Eggs are good value. Still twelve to the dozen.'

Any old bangers
A notice in the window of a car dealer's shop in St John's Wood lists cars under the headings: 'New' and 'Pre-owned'.

The new realism
A roadside sign at Bradwell, Norfolk, leaves nothing to the imagination. It says bluntly: 'Rabbits for sale, pets or meat.'

Sign in a yacht on display in a Hampshire boatyard: 'The shower door has been removed for your viewing pleasure.'

Helpmate
A reader reports that in one large San Francisco store Santa's grotto is now inhabited also by a large, determined-looking woman wearing spangles and a bustle. A store official gave him an official statement which read, in part: 'Why should Mrs Santa Claus have to stay on her own up at the North Pole every Christmas? Who can blame her if she decides to come along with old Santa?'

Fast movers
Sign on a stall in a London street market: 'Coloured athletic vests. Guaranteed not to run.'

Turkish delight
Extract from auction sale catalogue at Nether Wallop,

Hampshire: 'Lot 124. Hookah pipe. Adapted for electricity.'

A sticker seen in the back window of a car in Cromer this week urged: 'Buy British Footwear.' It would perhaps have been more influential had the car not been a Volvo.

Bottoms up
Notice seen in a furniture store:
> BARGAIN BASEMENT
> THIRD FLOOR

Ah, well
Seen advertised on a stall in a Birmingham market: 'Penny whistles: 60p each.'

Alex Day & Co, estate agents, had an advertisement in a recent edition of the Middlesex Chronicle *for a 'delightful semi-detached chalet type house enjoying views over large grass verge'.*

Paneful
An advertisement in the *Bromley Advertiser* proclaims: 'New Windows: Dramatic Breakthrough.'

Fill up
From a sign over a display of tinned sardines on a London market stall: 'Only 50p a tin! The oil alone is worth more!'

Switched on
Notice in the window of a travel agent in Edinburgh: 'Please do us a favour and go away.'

Be Warned!

Hitting the headlines
Sign on the back of a newsagent's van seen on the M3 near Basingstoke: 'Don't drive too close or you may end up in the papers.'

Step on it
A sticker on a car seen in south-west London: 'God give me patience – but hurry!'

Only when accompanied
A notice on the locked door of Clatworthy church, West
Somerset, which is in need of repair, says: 'Entry is dan-
gerous except at the time of divine service.'

Be unprepared
Notice in a staff canteen in Basingstoke: 'Please note that
there will be a surprise fire alarm at 10am next Friday.'

Mind your toes
I have mentioned several warnings recently which would
seem to be a bit unnecessary, like 'Give way to trains' and
'Do not molest the alligators'. I now hear from a Cali-
fornian beauty spot where a vast chunk of stone, probably
all of fifty tons, lies near the edge of a cliff.
    On this an anonymous hand has inscribed: 'Do not try
to shift this rock.'

That figures
At a village fete in Speen, Berkshire, it was announced that
the display by the Free Fall Parachute Team would be
followed by a St John Ambulance demonstration.

Over the top
Notice in a Soho club window: 'Topless Bar – Cover
charge £1.'

*Forewarning notice seen in the casualty department of a
Dublin hospital: 'Have you tried prayer?'*

First thrust
Notice in the staff canteen at a Coventry factory: 'The
fencing club meets for instruction and practice in the games
room every Tuesday at 7pm. New blood always welcome.'

Fair warning
Sign over a snack bar in a Hampshire inn: 'Do not touch
the food.'

Caveat emptor
A sign seen in an Essex shoe shop window says: 'Always a
good selection of inexpensive shoes. Repairs same day.'

Making amens
Sign on a garage door next to St Jude's Church, South
Kensington: 'No parking. Trespassers will be prayed for.'

Grave warning
Sign at the entrance to a Norfolk field: 'Trespassers will not be prosecuted. Next of kin will be informed.'

Tail piece
A tourist in Devon reports seeing a sign on a gate leading to a piece of tent-tempting land: 'Trespassers are requested not to play with the adders.'

In Response

The retort courteous

Sign of the times
After a visit to the dentist, a young girl placed her extracted tooth under her pillow on going to bed.

'Do you still believe in fairies?' asked her mother.

'No', she replied. 'But I still believe in Daddy.'

The hard stuff
A Sheffield reader – and a Liberal, too – reports seeing in a book shop's tray of remainders a work called *Dredging in Deep Water*. He said to the assistant: 'Surely you're going to have difficulty in clearing that one?'

'Oh, no, it'll go', she replied. 'After all, we sold one yesterday on Liberal policy.'

The more the merrier
'People who drink too much should be treated by a doctor', proclaims a scrawl in a Camberwell pub. Under it someone has written: 'People who drink too much don't mind who treats them.'

The autumn issue of the Gallipoli Association's journal, The Gallipolian, *reproduces the reply a veteran of the campaign claims to have sent after a long letter from his landlord seeking to end his tenancy. 'Dear Sir, I remain, yours faithfully . . .'*

Illegal entry?
A lawyer tells of a form he once received which included the question: 'Are you a natural born British subject?' His client had replied: 'No, by Caesarian operation.'

55

The quip modest

Mot juste
The Government of Uganda recently asked the World Bank to find someone to work in an undefined capacity for President Amin. The bank found a suitable recruit, an Englishman, and cabled him an offer, adding: 'You have a prepaid cablegram of twenty-four letters in which to reply.'

In precisely twenty-four letters his reply was: 'HA HA HA HA HA HA HA HA HA HA HA HA.'

The better of it
From the Royal Marines' 45 Commando comes a story of Belfast people taunting a police cordon with calls of, 'We're on rent and rates strike, we're on rent and rates strike'.

After a pause, the policemen retorted in kind: 'We're on time and a half, we're on time and a half!'

And/or Madams
A colleague has been rebuked by a female official of a 'radical' group for opening his letter to them with the words 'Dear Sirs'. He has pointed out in reply that signing his letter 'Yours faithfully,' did not necessarily mean he had any faith in their organisation.

Economic forecast
'What do you think of the Post Office troubles?' – 'They'll be printing £1 notes with glue on the back next year.'

The reproof valiant

One in the eye
A champagne-loving friend of mine offered help as a British Airways stewardess wrestled with a recalcitrant cork. 'I suppose you're an expert', she said haughtily as she refused and struggled on.

'Well', he bridled, 'I am actually a Chevalier of a champagne order'.

'Yes', she came back, 'but I am insured if I put a passenger's eye out with the cork – and you are not'.

Ask a silly . . .
A teacher at a special school in Buckinghamshire, talking to his children about numbers, time and clocks, finally posed the question: 'What has two arms, a face and keeps

telling you something?' After a moment one of his boys asked: 'How do you spell teacher?'

Car crazy
A reader whose young daughter is forever asking for lifts in the family car tells me she admonished her the other day by saying: 'What do you think the Almighty gave us two legs for?'

Her daughter replied: 'One for the brake and one for the accelerator.'

The countercheck quarrelsome

So there!
When a Hampshire reader asked a local shopkeeper if he had got the two gallons of paint she had ordered a week previously and he said 'No', she protested vehemently and asked him how he ever expected to do any business.

'Listen, madam,' he replied, 'if you are going to be nasty about it I won't even bother to send off the order'.

A Cheshire reader who asked directory inquiries for the number of a firm called Alpha Cleaning Services was told they were not listed, until he spelled out the name. He then got the number with the rebuke: 'If it's not spelled normally you are meant to tell us, you know!'

Sterling service
Two visitors came into a café in a West Sussex village and ordered tea, one with milk and the other with lemon. The waitress told them they could have the tea with lemon if they went into the shop next door and bought one.

Knowing his rights
From the Isle of Man comes the tale of an impeccably logical response by a visitor who refused to contribute to a Royal National Lifeboat Institution collection on the grounds: 'Oh, I flew over.'

When a woman passenger on a 137 bus in London complained about the irregularity of the service, she got this graceful reply from an inspector: 'Get a taxi!'

Catch as catch can
There is still little love lost between provincial police forces and Scotland Yard. George Oldfield, Assistant Chief Constable of West Yorkshire, in charge of finding the North

Country murderer who calls himself 'Jack the Ripper', was asked if he was going to call in the Yard.

'Why should I' he growled. 'They haven't caught their's yet.'

Passage to Hampstead
Wishing to go from Tottenham Court Road to Hampstead Heath, a reader boarded a No 24 bus whose destination blind proclaimed 'Oxford Circus'. When asked where it was going, the conductor said 'Hampstead Heath', and when told of the blind, he replied: 'There is India on the tyres but we're not going to Calcutta.'

A Few Wonders of Science

Chain reaction
The old injunction against pulling the chain while the train is in the station has now found its place in the nuclear age. At the University of Florida, scientists are confronted by a notice reading: 'Please don't flush toilet while reactor is running.'

The reactor's cooling system, it seems, draws water from the same supply and malfunctions when the flow is diverted to flush the toilet.

In the Andover Advertiser *a firm is offering fuel economy ideas under the heading: 'Use your head . . . Burn wood!'*

Eavesdropping
The Rev Kenneth Lucas, Rector of St Mary's, West Chiltington, Sussex, offers a word of warning to technology buffs. At a wedding ceremony recently, one of the guests recorded the vows on his sophisticated tape equipment. So sensitive, indeed, was the microphone that it not only picked up all the official words of the service but also the clergyman's whispered advice to the bridegroom who was having difficulty sliding the ring on to his bride's finger – 'Spit on it!'

Local authorities which have reglazed the windows of their public lavatories with unbreakable glass to make them 'vandal proof' now face a new hazard. A reader tells me that one aspiring hooligan chucked a stone at the tough new glass causing the missile to rebound and hit him in the face. His irate mother then threatened to sue the council for injuring her child.

The lavatory at the Green Isle Hotel in Clondalkin, I learn from the Irish Times, *lies beyond a door marked 'Toilets'. You are then faced with three doors, one marked 'Ladies', one 'Gentlemen' and the third, 'Switchroom'.*

From England I now hear of the research department in a local factory where, at the end of a corridor, were three doors marked 'Ladies', 'Gentlemen' and 'Experimental'.

More or less
Overheard on a building site where two labourers were estimating a length of water pipe: 'Well, it's about a metre, plus a foot.'

An elderly lady tried to ring her son at his office and was greeted by his voice on a telephone answering machine saying: 'Please leave your message . . .' When he returned, he found his tape had recorded her exasperated voice saying: 'Brian, this is your mother. If you keep saying that to me any more I'll not speak to you again.'

Craftsmanship
A man, consulting his watch as he looked at a sundial at Durlston Castle, was heard to say: 'Not bad after 100 years – only about an hour slow.'

Overheard in the RAF *Club: 'When I saw the pictures of all the desolation on Mars I had a nasty feeling that perhaps man had already been there.'*

What Was That Again?

Society portrait
Jim Murphy, headmaster of a comprehensive school in the Staffordshire town of Kidsgrove, and President of the National Union of Teachers, gave his union's conference in Scarborough this description of contemporary Britain:
   'A pools win, sin bin, wimpy bar, two car, first name, loose dame, rolling stone, ansafone, loud sound, sleep around, disco scenes, tight jeans, colour telly, slingawelly, page threes, deep freeze, opt out, be a lout, dull void, unemployed type of society.'

Slight slip
Sign inside a dry-cleaner's at Calamayor, Majorca, spotted by a reader on holiday: 'Drop your trousers here for the best results.'

Long-haul passenger
Heard in Terminal 2 at Heathrow: 'Would Mr Seymour of Mars please go to the British Airways information desk.'

Depends what you mean
The first paragraph of a letter from the Ordnance Survey to various architects runs: 'In 1969 a standard licence fee for architects' practices was introduced . . . Since then the fee has remained unchanged apart from the price increases that have occurred over the years.'

A shopkeeper in Kilburn High Road yesterday shooed away a small boy begging 'Pennies for the Guy' in his doorway. 'You're far too early!' he cried, and then returned into his shop to continue his job of putting up his Christmas decorations.

Overseas initiative
A woman who called at the BBC overseas department and asked for the Urdu section was directed by the commissionaire to a ladies' hairdresser – for an 'airdo.

Ready for the off
Sign in a Norfolk launderette: 'When others are waiting, please remove your clothes as soon as the light goes out.'

Those whom the gods . . .
I learned yesterday from a reader of a couple who answered an advertisement for a second-hand car and offered a £400 social security cheque in payment.

'We're supposed to use it to buy furniture', they explained. 'But everyone else seems to buy cars with the money. There'll be no problem over the cheque.'

Alas, there wasn't – it was honoured.

Seen pushing his car in Trafalgar Square in Tuesday night's pouring rain was an Admiral in full-dress uniform. At the wheel, in the dry, sat his Marine driver.

Yes, but whose?
Heading from a local paper: 'Tax Inspector Gives his 50th Pint of Blood.'

Penny a word?
Prominently displayed outside a bookshop in Cochin, South India, is a baffling notice: 'Spoken English sold here.'

Better address
Sign seen on a Leeds building: 'Chiropodist removed to Corn Exchange.'

Don't be L8
An advertising magazine in the Midlands, describing a shop's stock of military regalia says the most expensive item is the badge of a full colonel in the C4th Highlanders.

Ah, so Dai!
The programme of the Welsh Boxing Association's fiftieth anniversary gathering contains a huge slogan: 'Welsh, and proud of it – on behalf of the Sony Company.'

Did my ears deceive me, or was a visiting Arab prince said in a news bulletin to have held a 'working banquet?'

Can you call back?
Several readers were intrigued by the week-end BBC radio news report of the siege of the French Embassy in San Salvador which began: 'All attempts to contact the guerrillas have proved fruitless. It seems they have taken the phone off the hook . . .'

So I should hope
From an army list of resettlement vacancies: 'Ejection-seat tester . . . small amount of travelling involved.'